Friendship:
Understanding Connections

Heather N. Croas

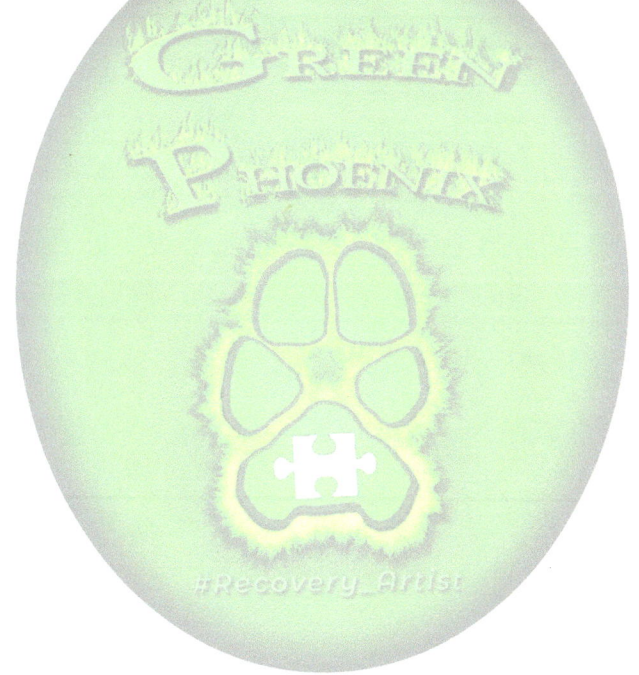

This book is dedicated to Pastor Jennifer Grawey whose continued support and encouragement not only inspired this project but also helped it become a reality. Thank you for helping me understand the importance of connection, community and friendship.

This project was initially created for someone who has helped me gain a better understanding of what friendship and healthy relationships looks like. My goal was to create a series of photos to illustrate what I've learned because finding the right words to express the thoughts and emotions is difficult.

The first series of photos features a pair of old and tattered shoes on a well-worn path. The goal is for people to see that this friend has walked their own path and knows how hard it can be. And now she is helping me walk my own path one step at a time because she knows what it's like to struggle through it.

Having someone in your life who has walked a similar path and knows the struggles can be an invaluable resource. While they may not be able to completely understand what you're going through knowing that they've faced their own struggles and have been able to make it to other side provides a sense of hope.

When someone who has walked through and survived their own wilderness is willing to reach back and help you find your own path, it makes it a little easier to navigate through the obstacles that can cause you to stumble and fall.

Sometimes it can be hard to continue fighting when it feels like there is no way out. But seeing the worn-out shoes that have blazed the trail ahead provides the guidance and encouragement to keep going.

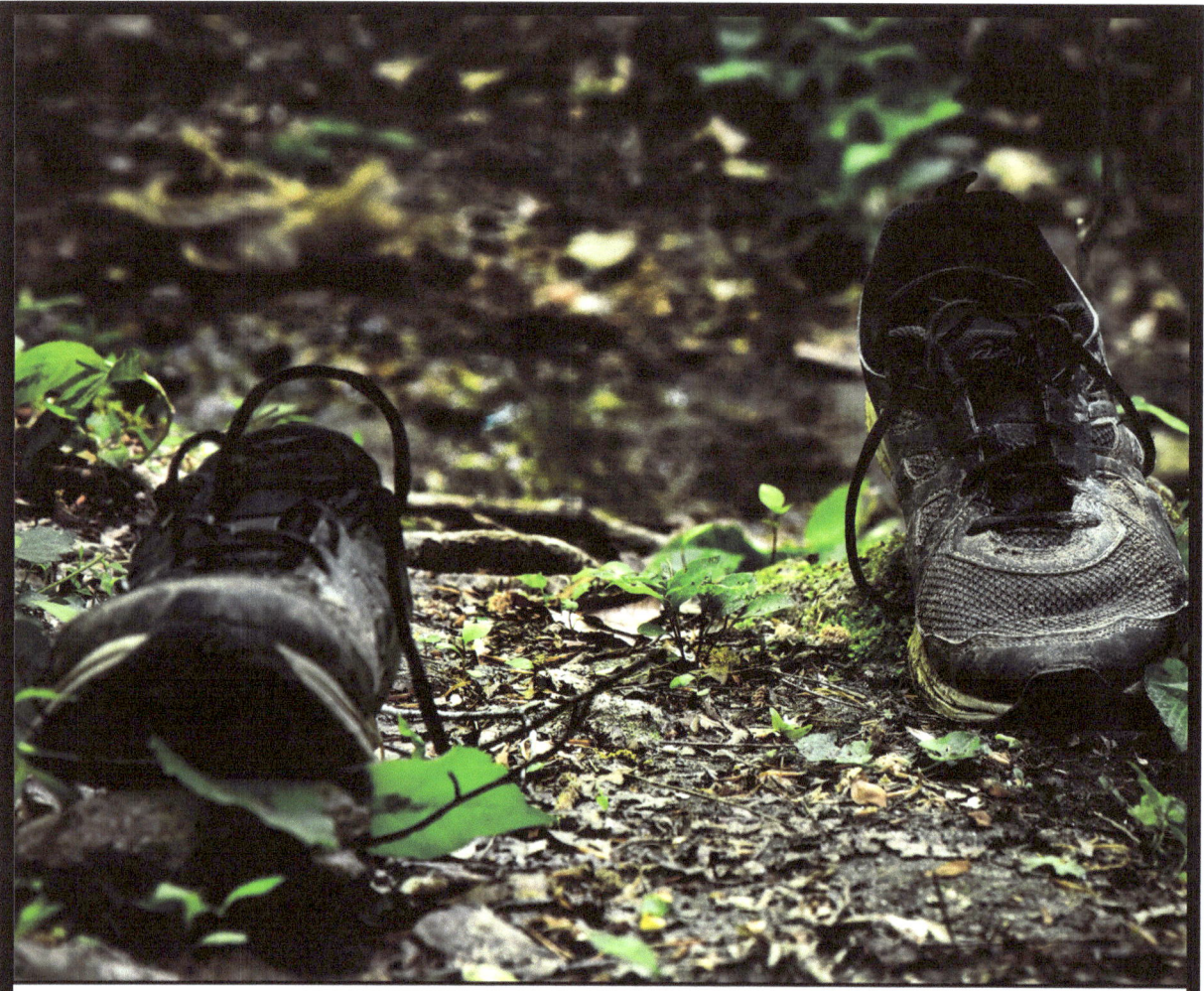

Having someone in your life who has lived through similar circumstances and is willing to walk alongside you as you navigate your own path is one of the priceless gifts that true friendship provides.

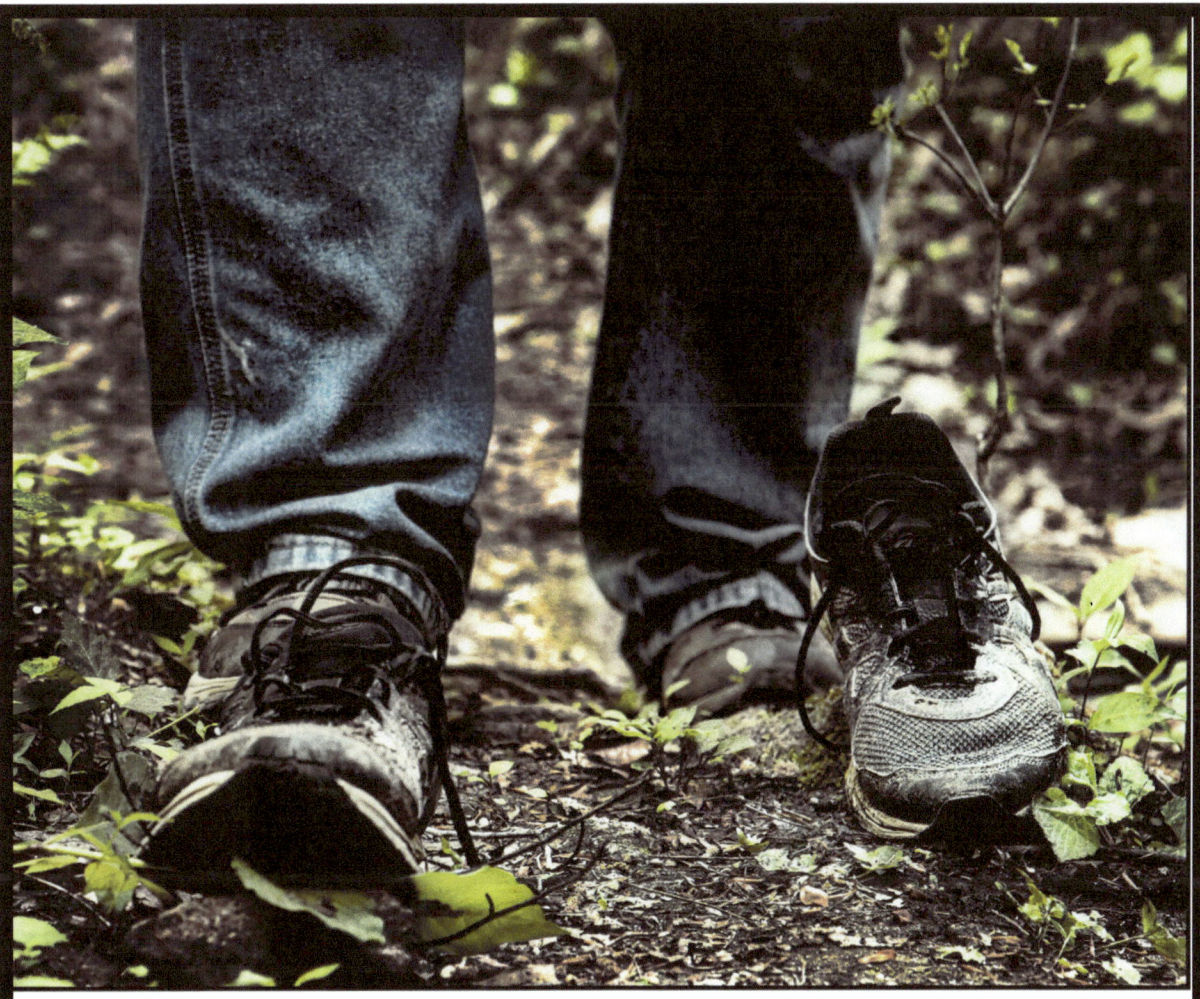

Knowing that they have lived through and survived a similar journey can provide the encouragement and support needed to continue your own.

Especially when they're willing to walk through it with you.

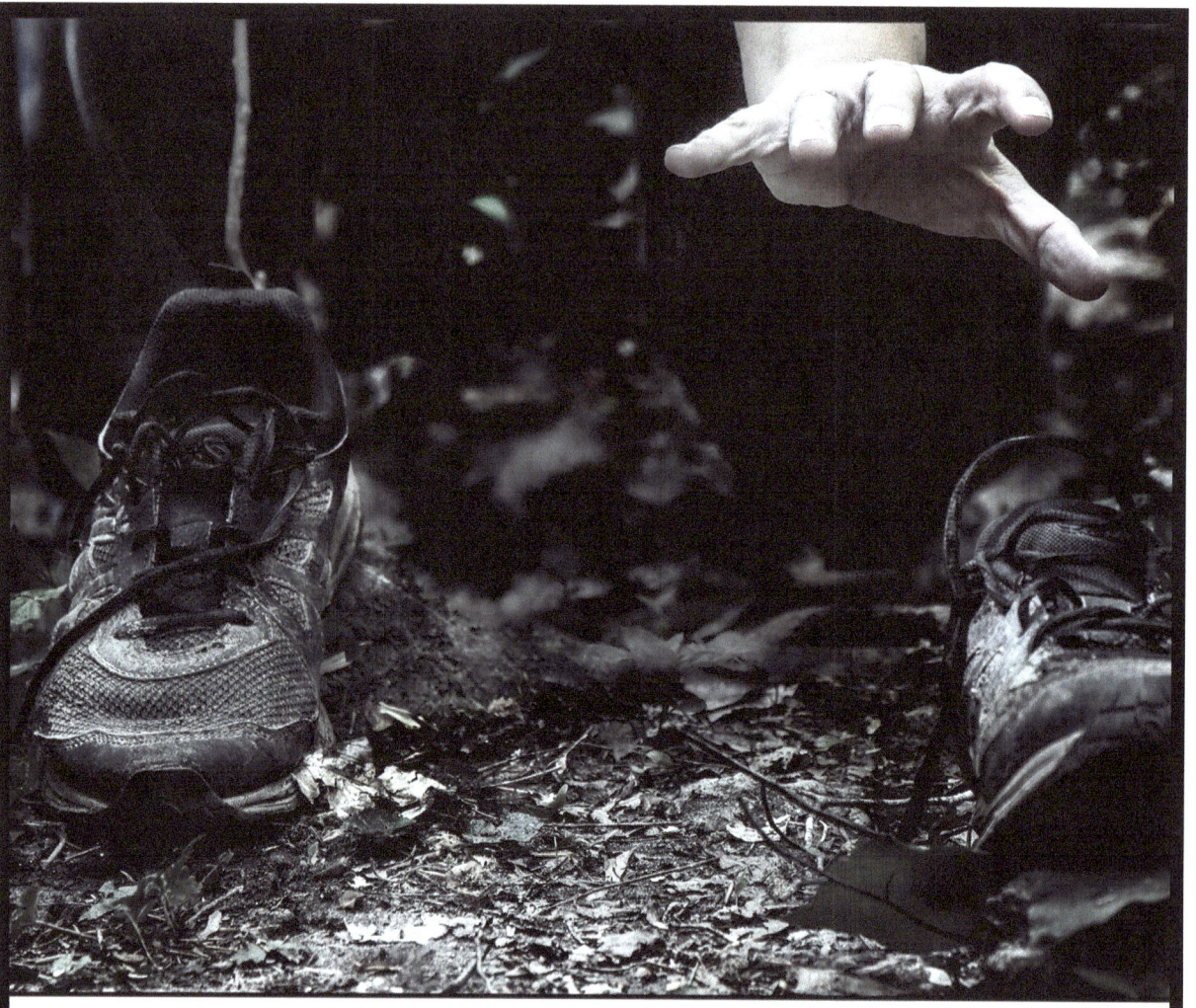

A sense of purpose and belonging are important as we were created to live in community.

But learning how to reach out for the support we need can be challenging at times.

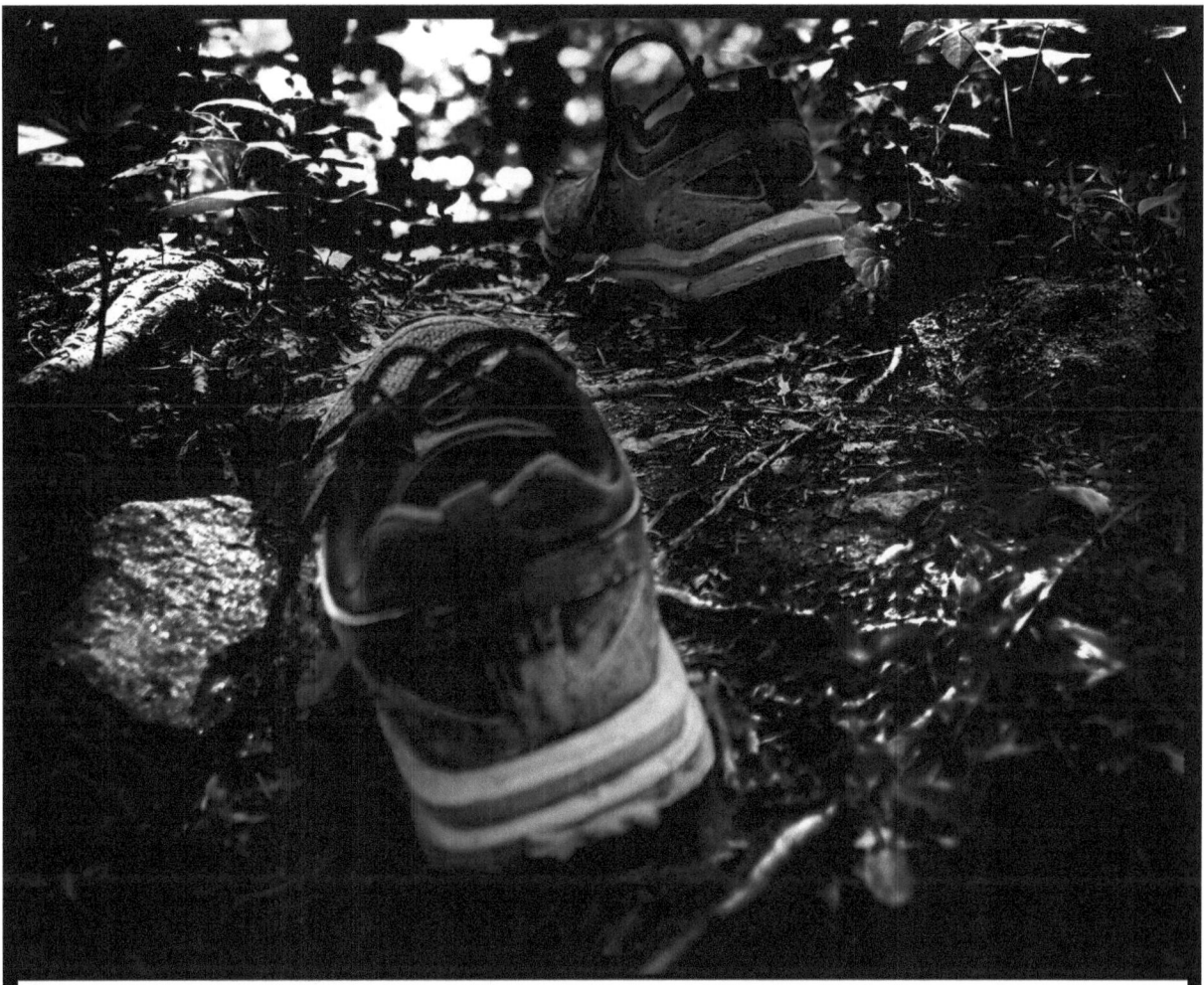

Having someone in your life who has lived through similar circumstances and is willing to walk alongside you as you navigate your own path is one of the priceless gifts that true friendship provides.

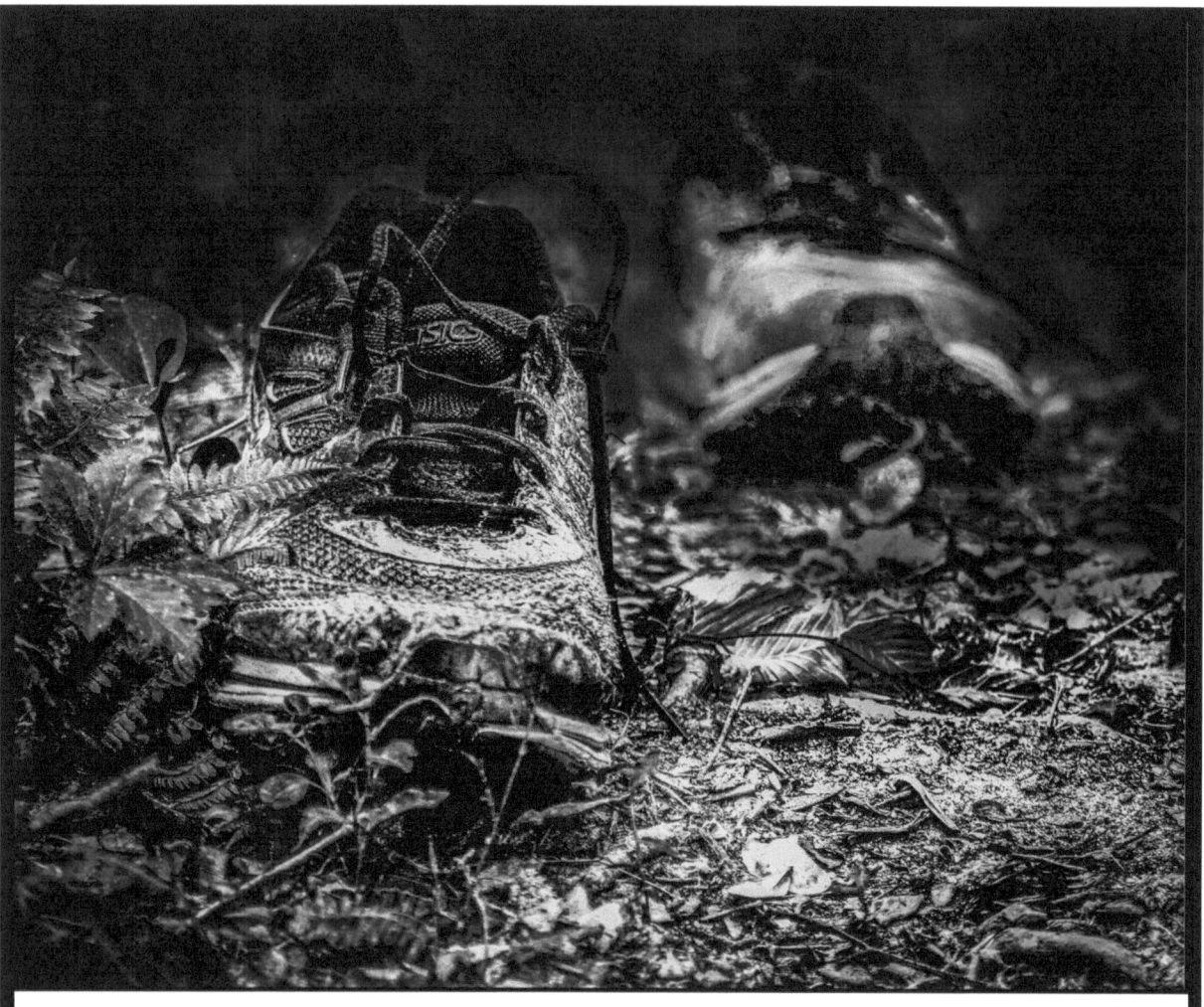

Having someone in your life who has lived through similar circumstances and is willing to walk alongside you as you navigate your own path is one of the priceless gifts that true friendship provides.

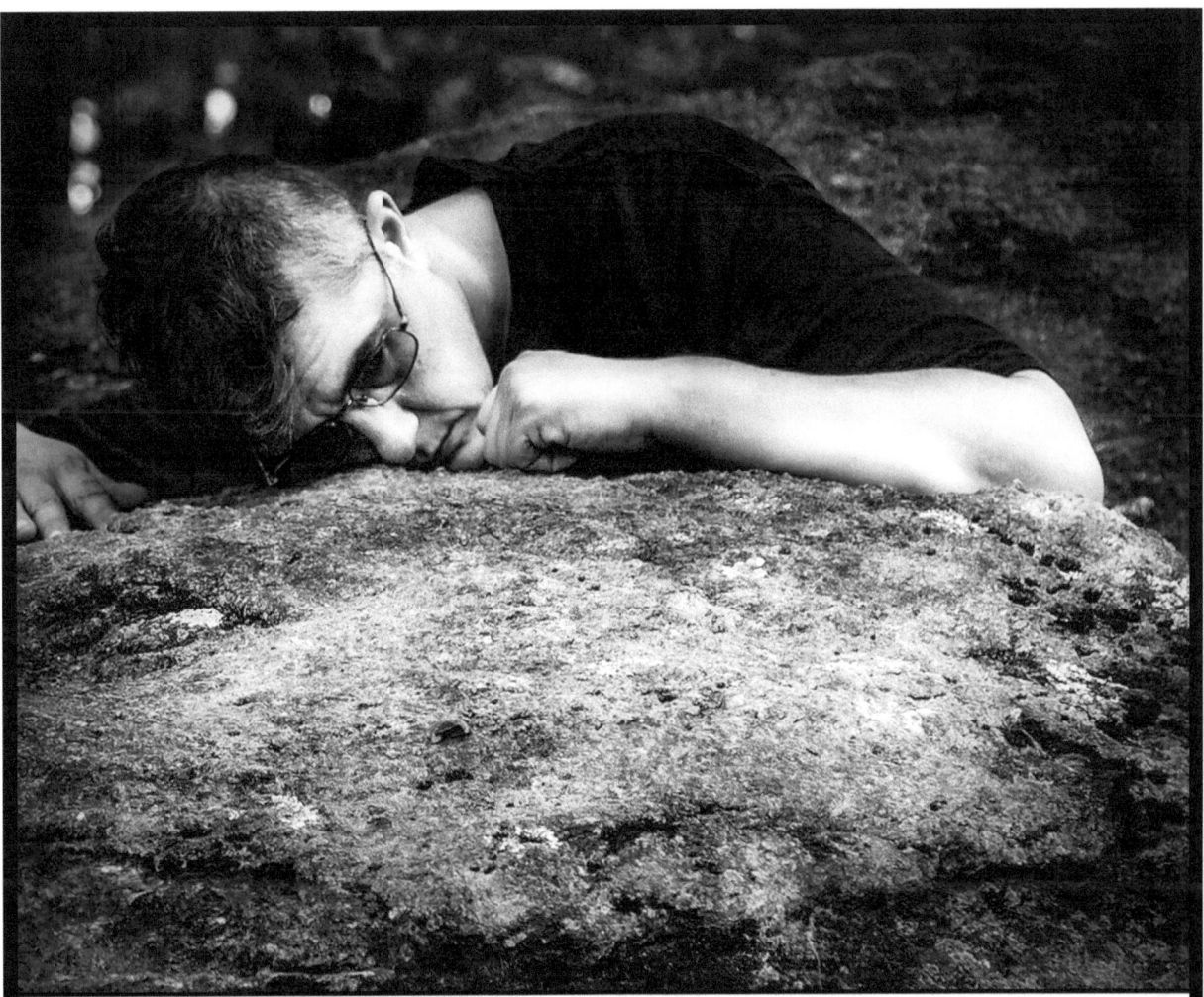

At some point in our lives, we find ourselves stuck between a "rock and a hard place".

But what if that rock is the person who is willing to stick with you through the hard places?

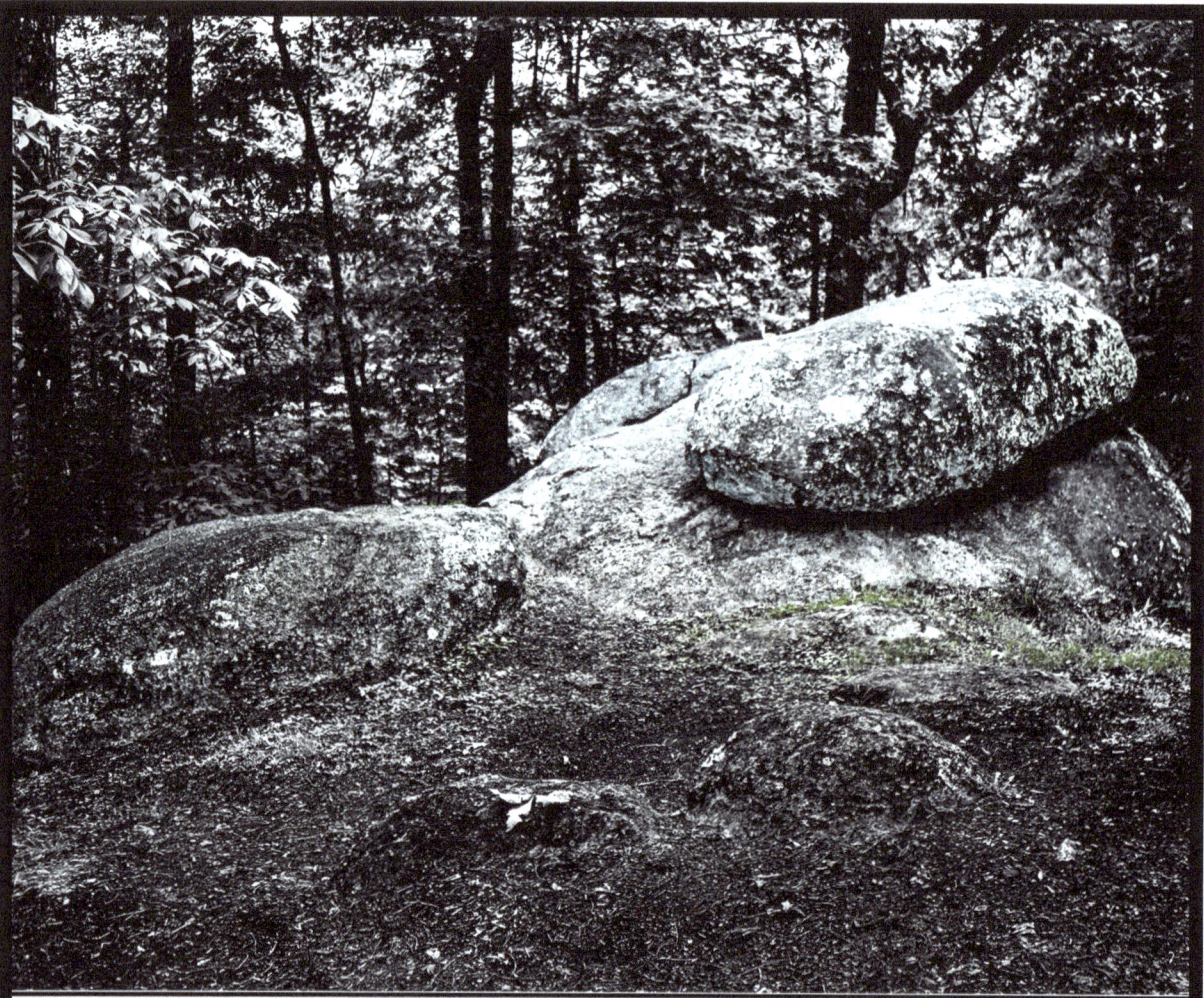

I was lucky enough to find someone who has been my "rock".

She has been there with me through the rough spots, and she doesn't move easily so it was important to find a big rock to illustrate her stubbornness and refusal to let me go.

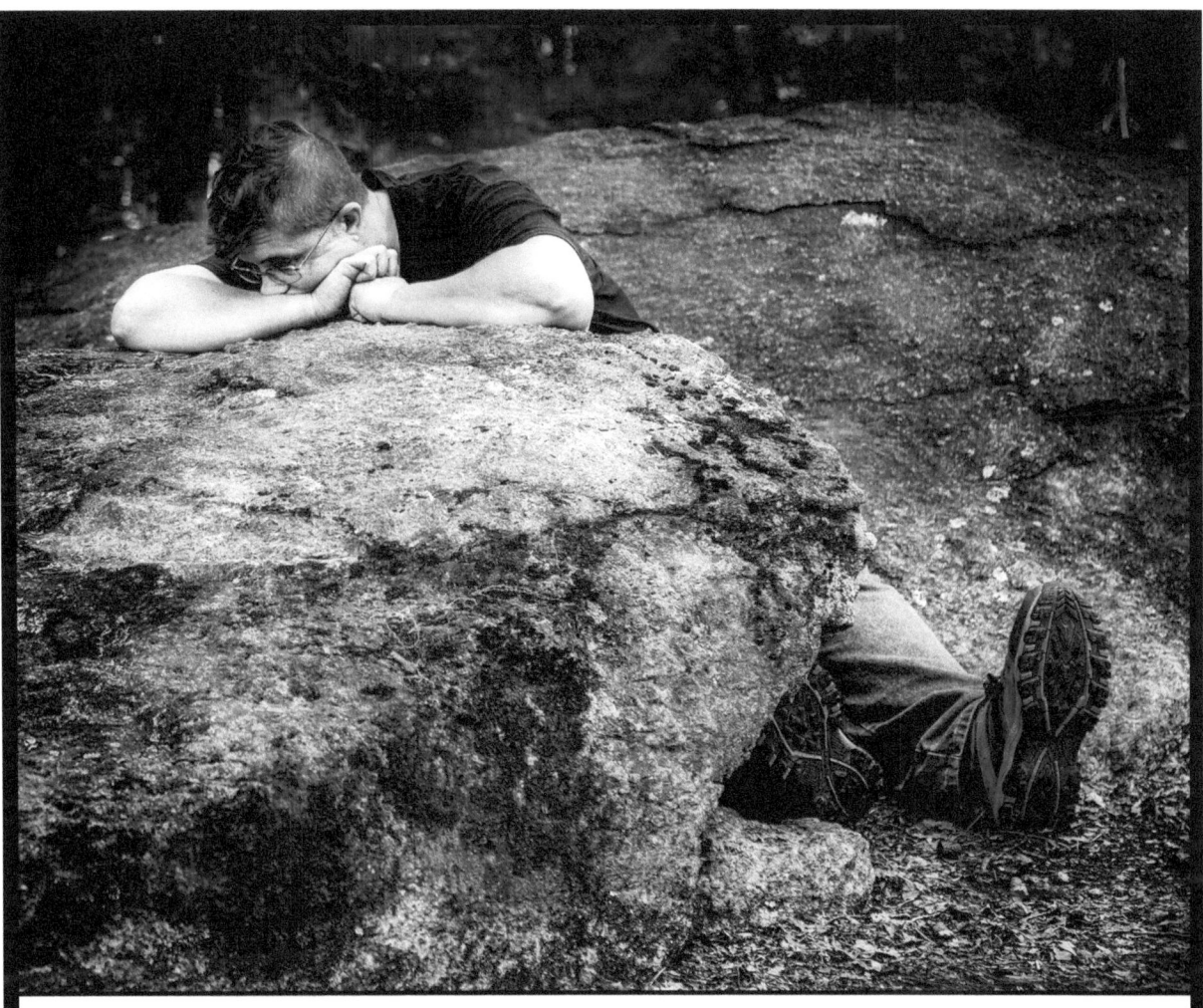

She's helped keep me grounded and provided the support I needed, letting me lean into her and providing me shelter from the storms of life.

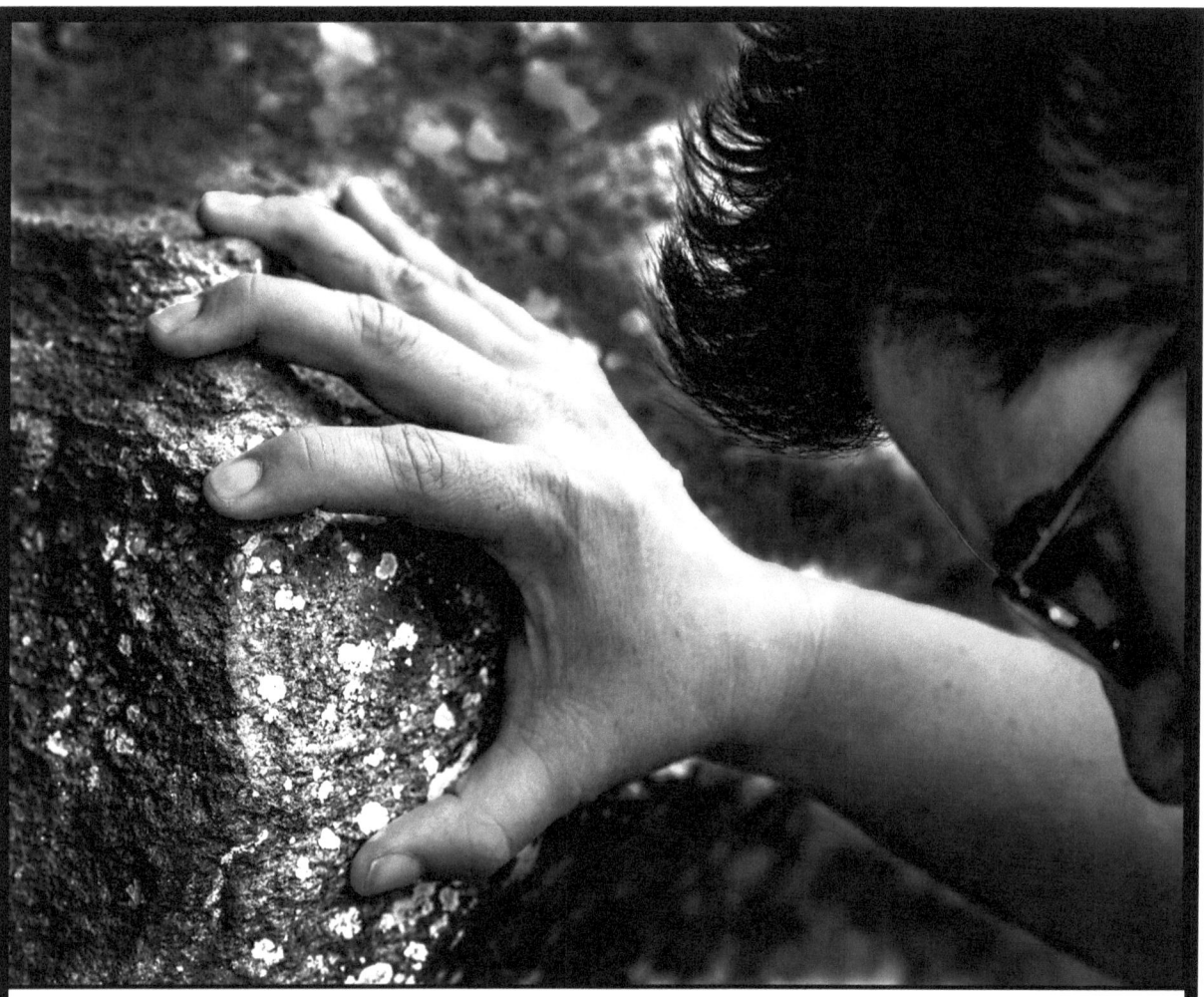

There have been times when I wanted to run away and hide but I found myself reaching out instead.

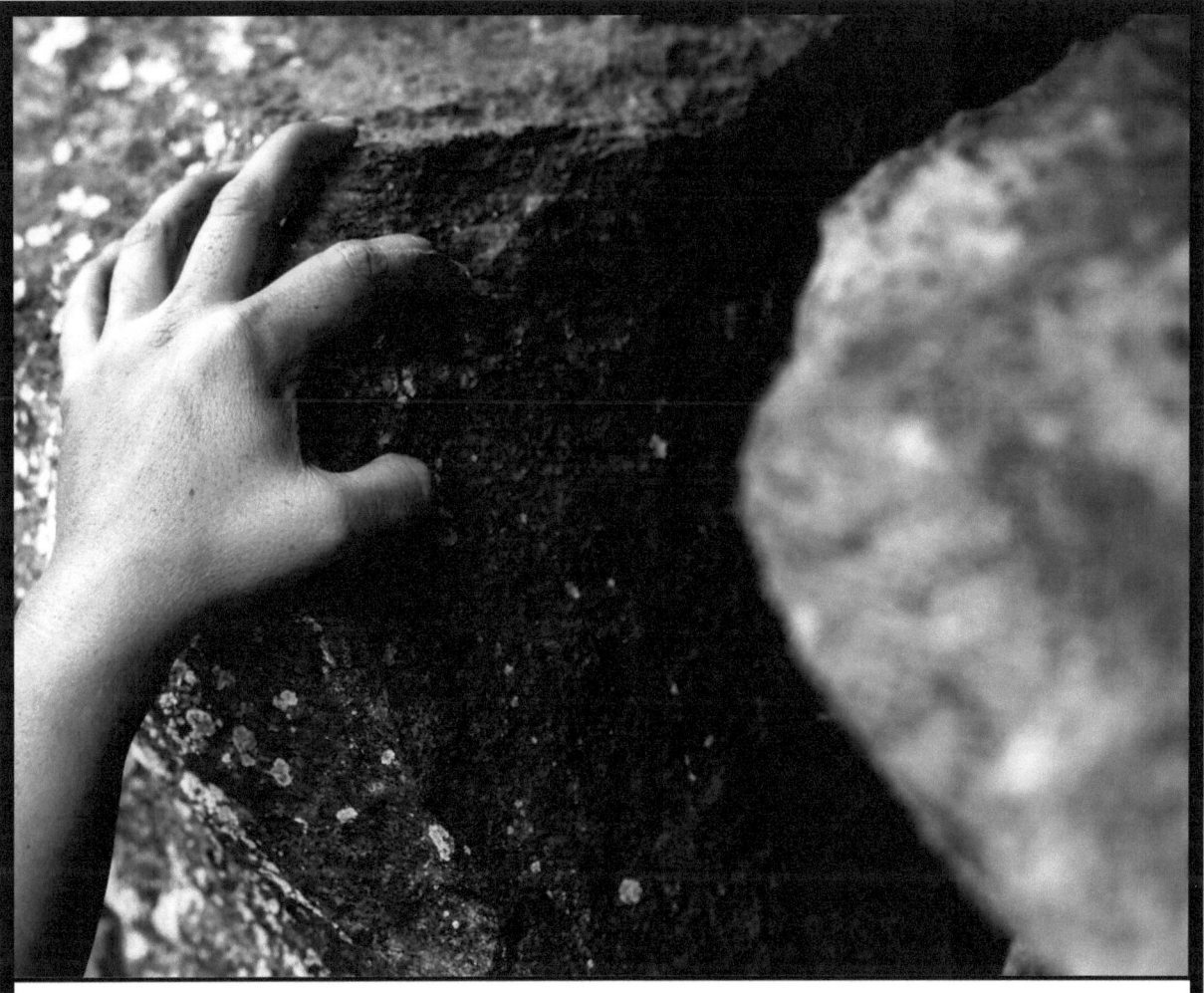

Especially during the times when I felt myself slipping back into the darkness...

She was there providing me the support I needed and something solid to hold on to.

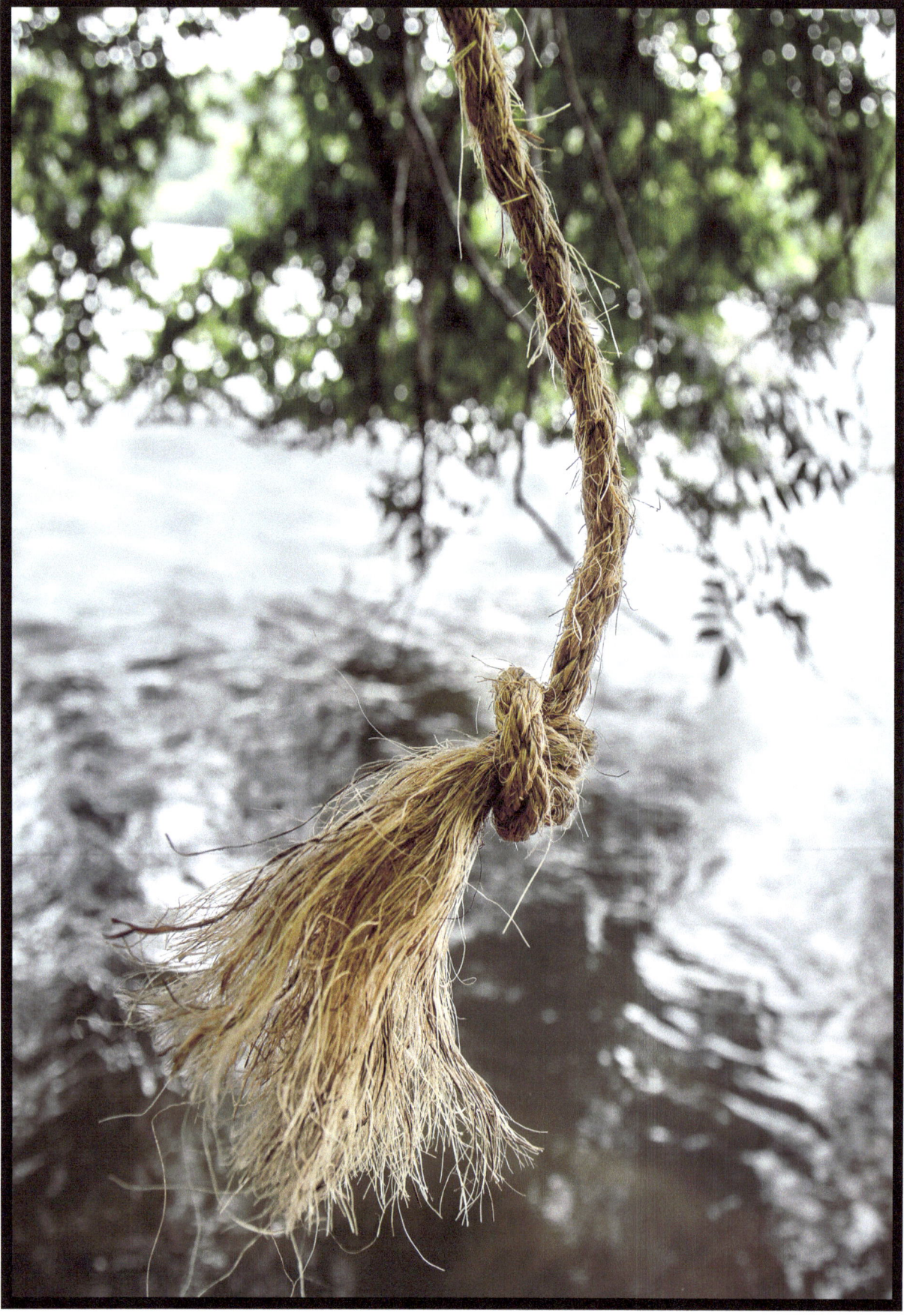

There are times in life when things become overwhelming.

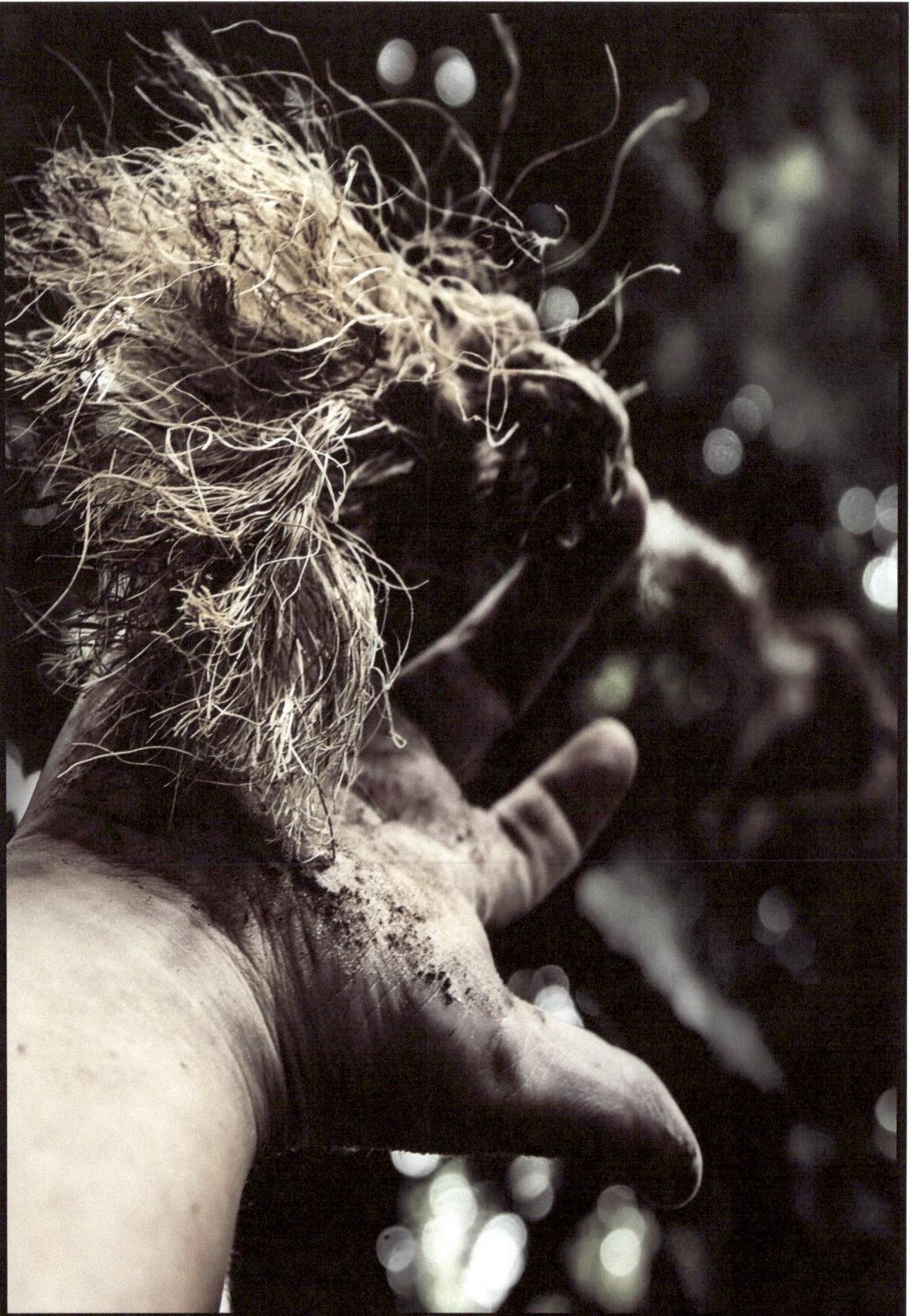

You get to the end of your rope and as hard as you try, you feel yourself slipping away.

That's when you need a friend to help you.

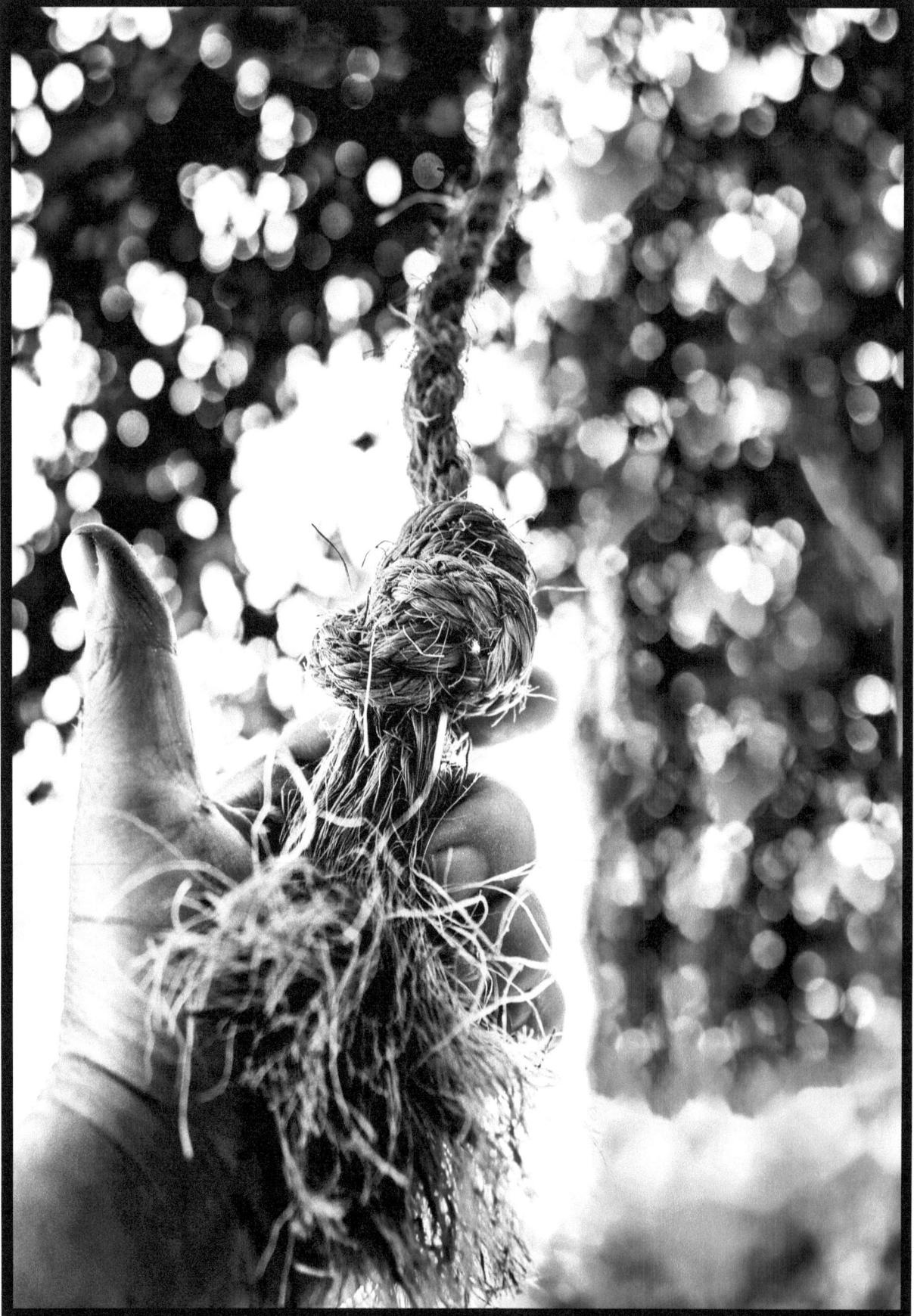

Sometimes you're trying hard to find something, anything to hold on to and a good friend provides you that something.

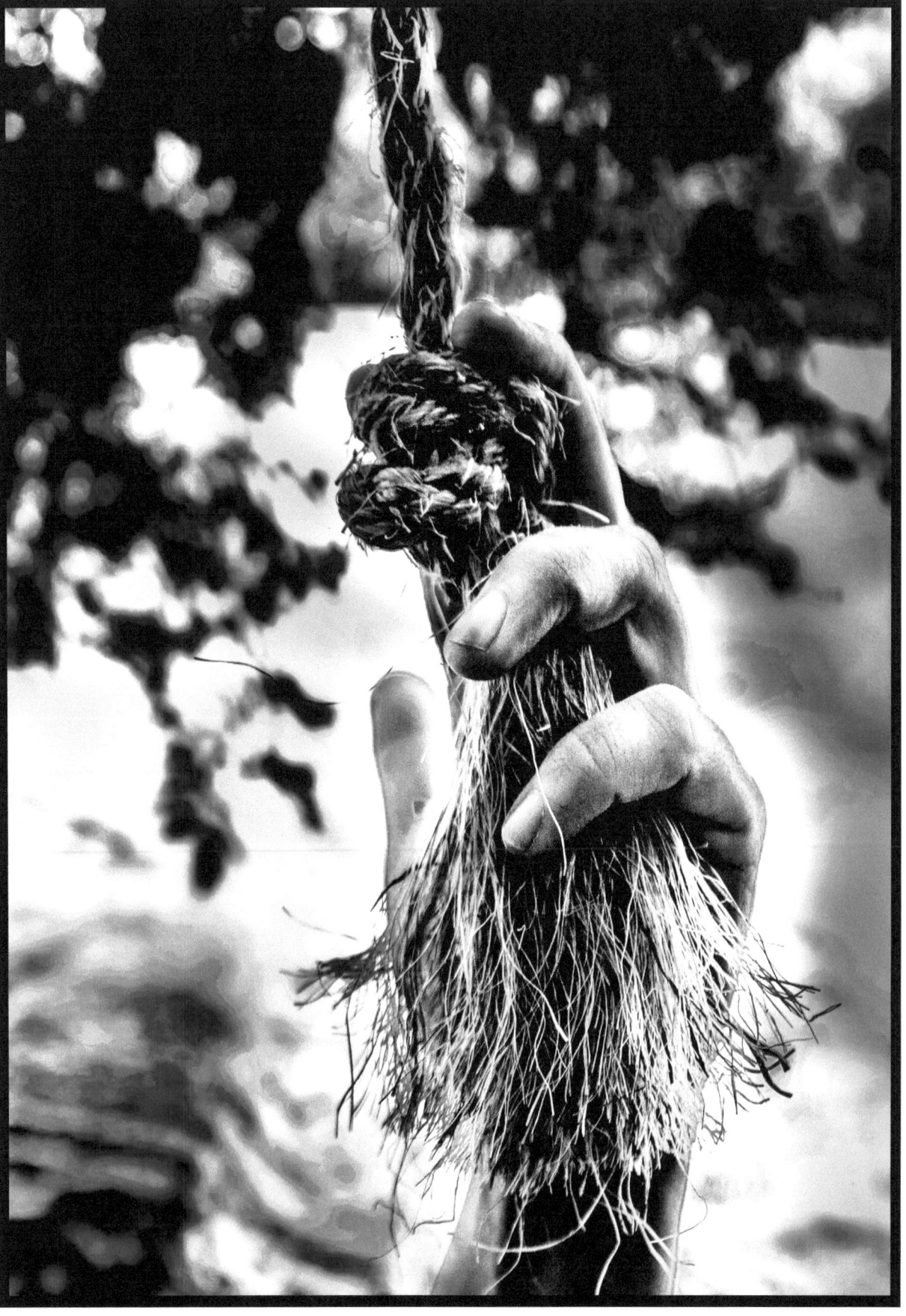

They're the ones who can tie a knot at the end and give you something to hold on to.

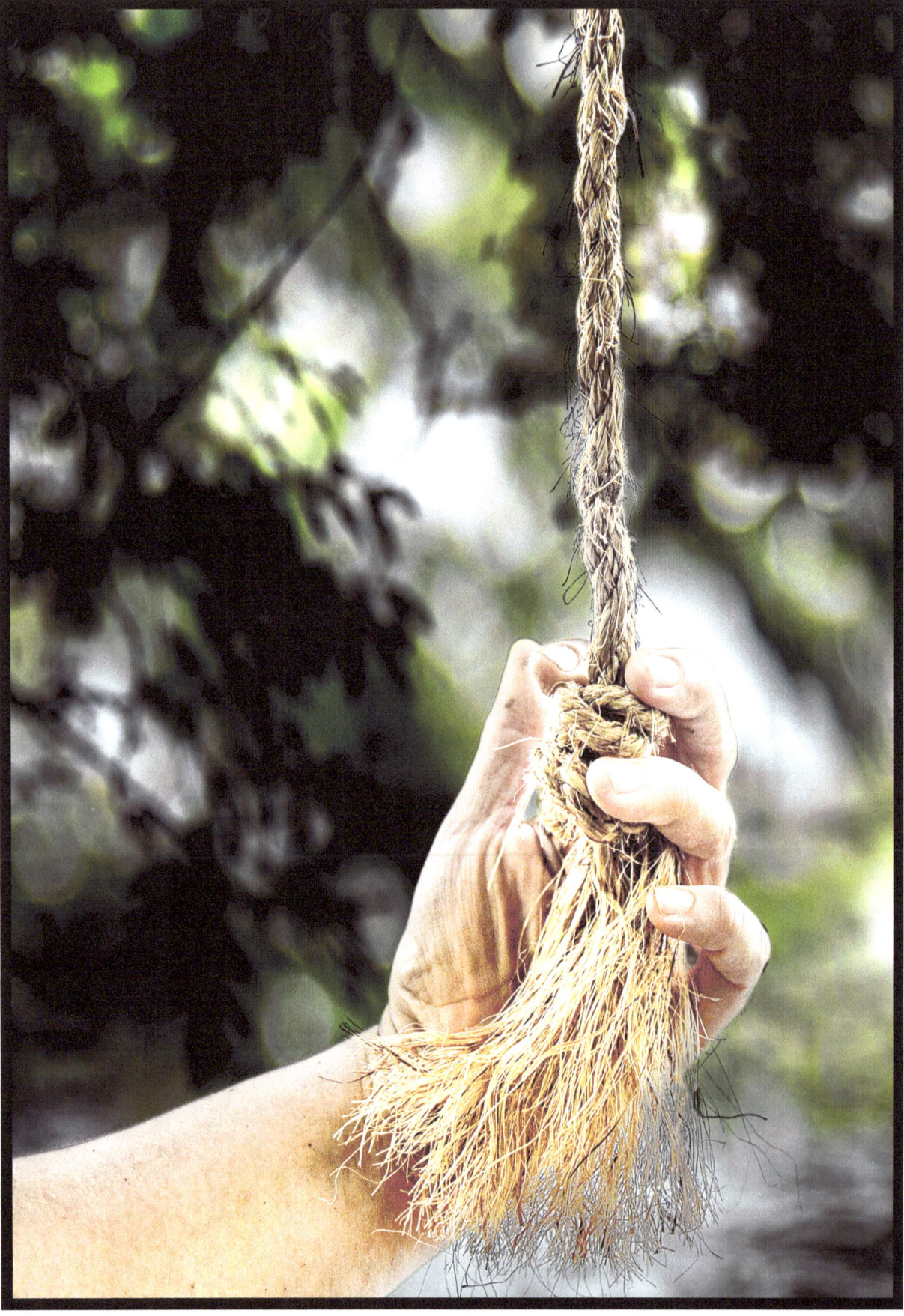

She's taught me that connection is important. We need help when we feel like we can't hang on and we want to just let go and give up.

Those connections are the key…
the friendships.

They're the knot that gives you something to cling to, the little extra support you need so your hand doesn't completely slip off.

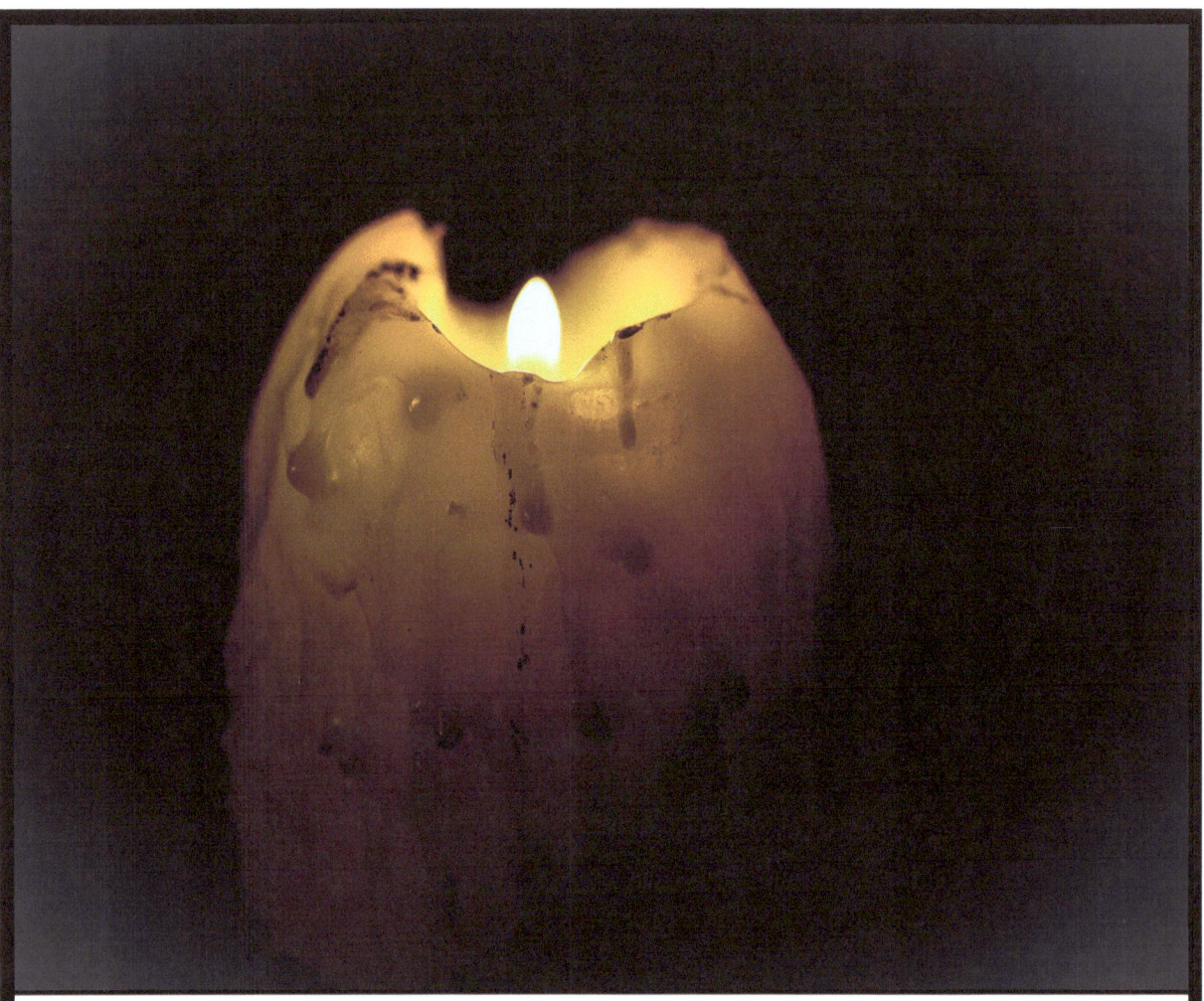

When you're surrounded by darkness it can be hard to search out the light. All too often there is a fear that the light at the end of the tunnel is an oncoming train bringing more pain and confusion.

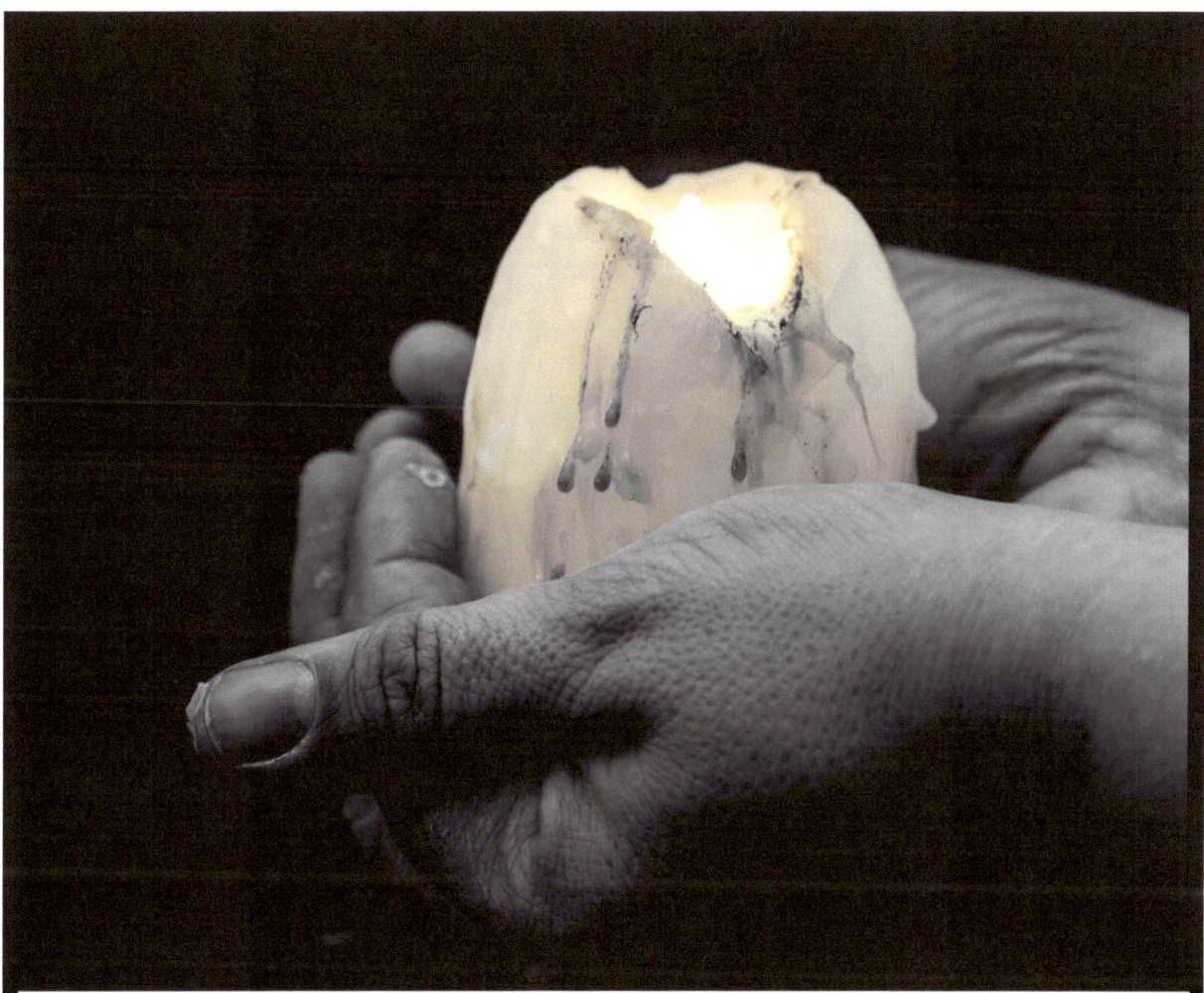

But over the last few years I've been fortunate enough to have a friend who has shown me that the light can also be comforting when it comes from a place of love.

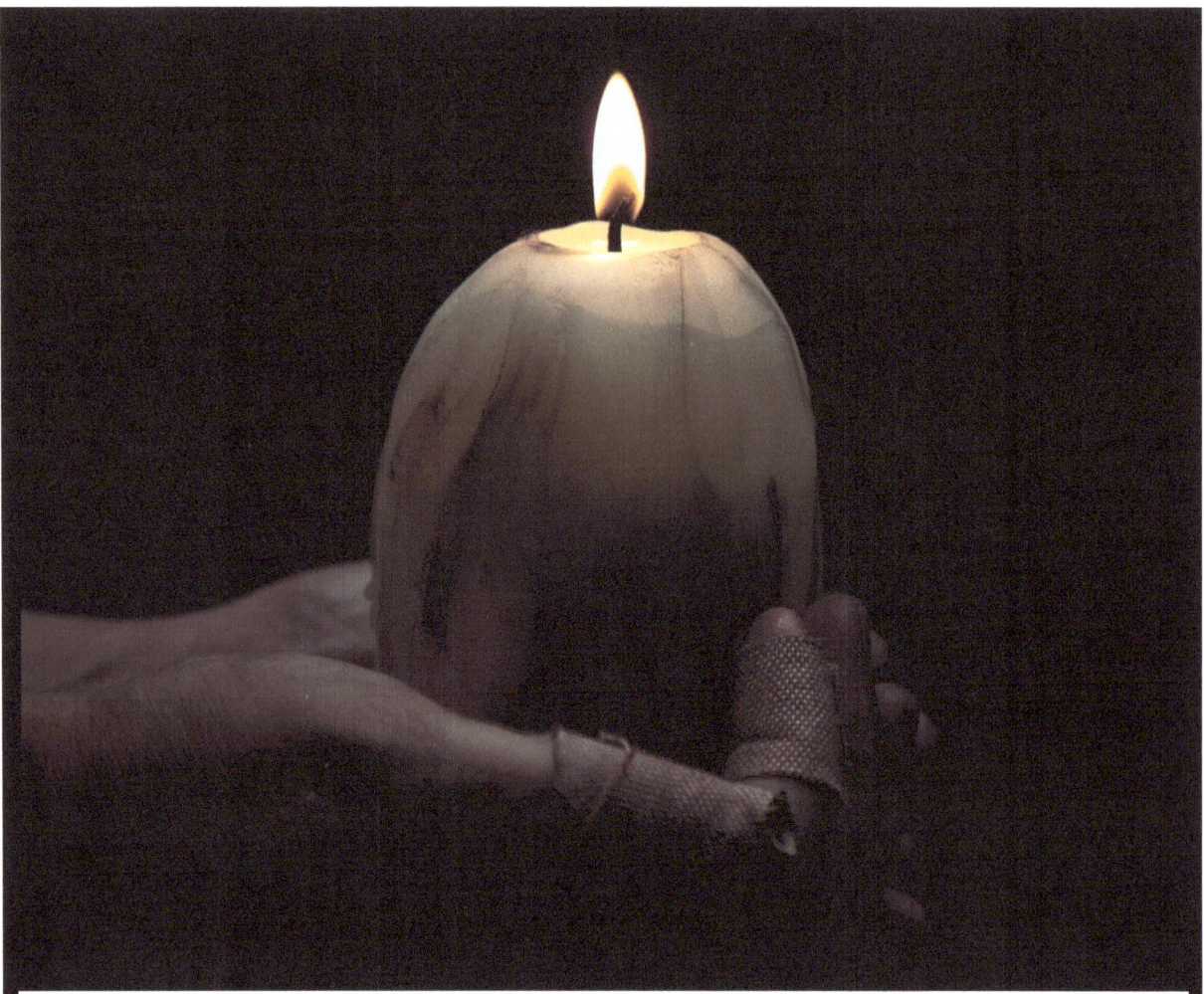

She has helped me to find a light piercing through the darkness. Not like a flashlight that can be bright and overwhelming but the gentle flame of a candle that slowly lights up the room.

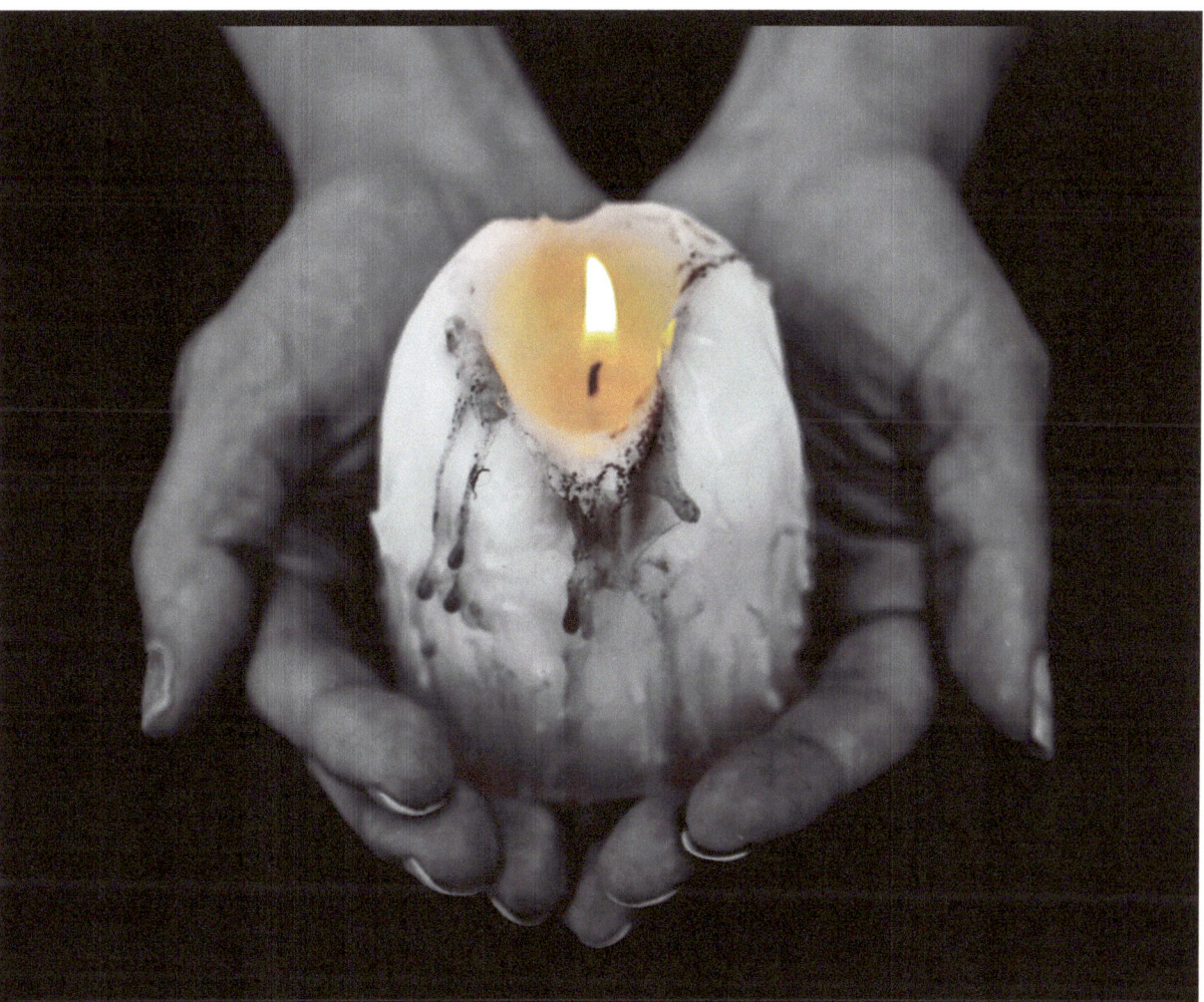

It's warm and comforting and not overly intimidating.

She's one of the people that has helped me find comfort by teaching about the true light of the world.

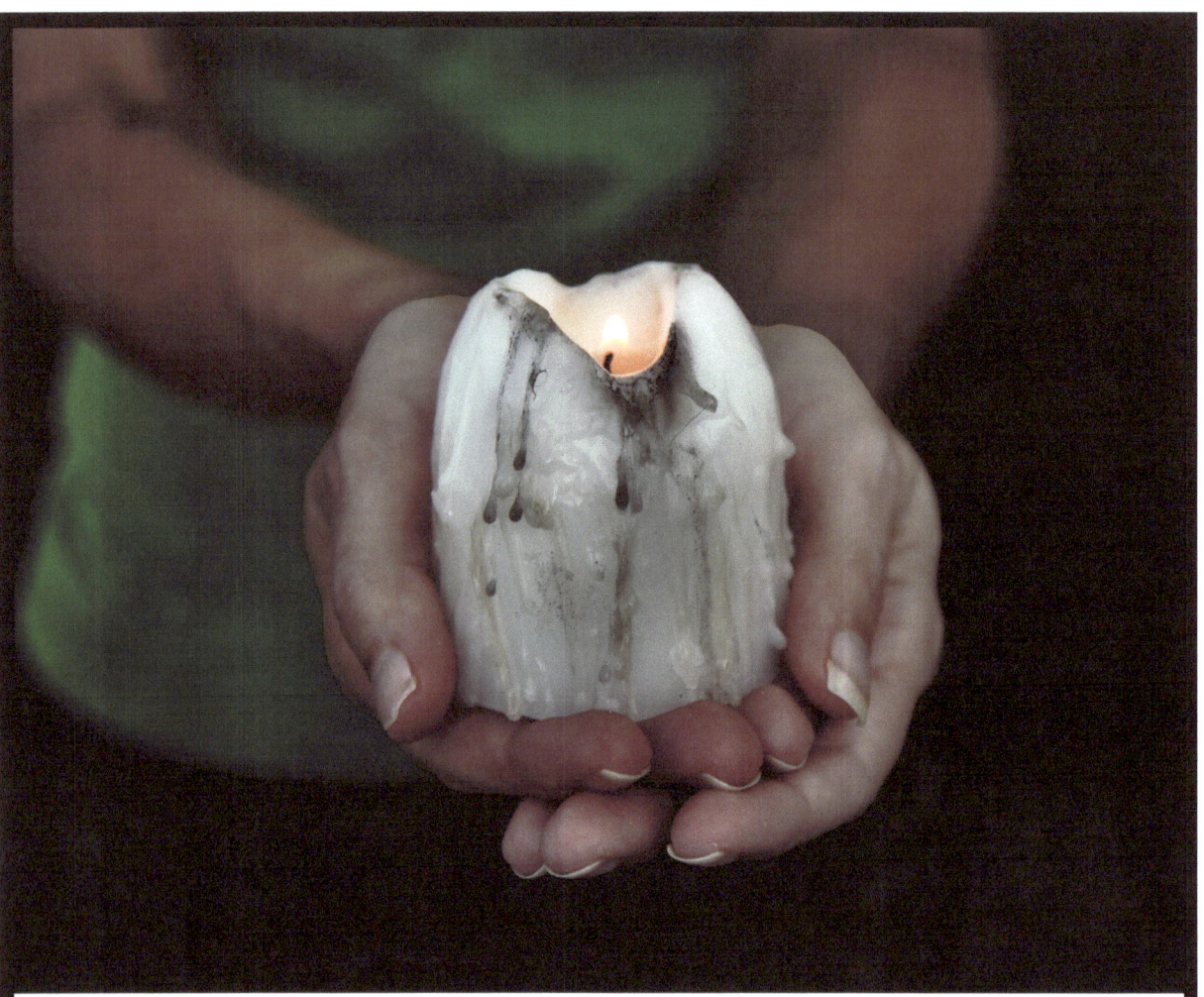

Friendship isn't easy and it gets messy sometimes.

It requires a commitment and willingness to work at it, especially when things get hard. But when we have a good friend, it helps us through the hard things we face in life.

One of the greatest lessons she's taught me is that everyone needs a friend.

www.ingramcontent.com/pod-product-compliance
Lightning Source LLC
Chambersburg PA
CBHW051830210526
45473CB00005B/1808